NO ORDINARY LOVE

MY JOURNEY FROM PUPPY LOVE
TO EXTRAORDINARY LOVE

KARIESHA TOPPING

© 2020 Divine Works Publishing LLC.

No Ordinary Love - My Journey from Puppy Love to Extraordinary Love

ALL RIGHTS RESERVED. No part of this publication may be reproduced, stored in a retrieval system, or transmitted in any form or by any means, electronic, mechanical, photocopying, recording or otherwise without the prior permission of the publisher or in accordance with the provisions of the Copyright, Designs, and Patents Act 1988 or under the terms of any license permitting limited copying issued by the Copyright Licensing Agency.

The views expressed in this work are solely those of the author and do not necessarily reflect the views of the publisher, the publisher hereby disclaims any responsibility for them.

Printed in the United States of America
First Edition: 2021

Scripture taken from the King James Version®., (unless otherwise noted), Copyright © 1982 by Thomas Nelson. Used by permission. All rights reserved.

ISBN 13: 978-1-949105-36-0 (Paperback)
ISBN 13: 978-1-949105-37-7 (Hardback)
ISBN 13: 978-1-949105-38-4 (eBook)

Published by:
Divine Works Publishing, LLC
Royal Palm Beach, Florida USA

www.DivineWorksPublishing.com
561-990-BOOK (2665)

Dedication

I dedicate this book to love!
After all, it's what inspired me to write it.

Contents

Dedication *vii*

Acknowledgments *xi*

Introduction *xiii*

Chapter 1 Growing up in Kingston, Jamaica *1*

Chapter 2 Migrating to the USA *3*

Chapter 3 Homesick *5*

Chapter 4 Returning to Jamaica *9*

Chapter 5 Love at First Sight *11*

Chapter 6 Adjusting to Life Abroad *15*

Chapter 7 Returning to Jamaica Again! *17*

Chapter 8 Puppy Love *19*

Chapter 9 First Kiss *21*

Chapter 10 Long Distance Love *23*

Chapter 11 Six Years Later *25*

Chapter 12 Grandpa's Funeral *29*

Chapter 13 Our Engagement *33*

Chapter 14 Our Wedding *37*

Chapter 15 Family of Three *41*

Chapter 16 Dream Big *45*

Chapter 17 My Queen *47*

Chapter 18 For Better or Worse *49*

Chapter 19 Love Letter to My Best Friend *57*

Chapter 20 My Prayer for You *59*

Acknowledgments

My husband, my best friend, cheers to us and a lifetime of happiness. My children, my two biggest motivators! So many times I felt like giving up on my dreams, but you guys push me to never give up. My parents, thank you for giving me life and mommy for passing your strength onto me. My brother, I love you no matter what! My sister, " my twin" I love you and stay strong in the lord. I saved the best for last, my Lord and Savior Jesus Christ without you this would not be possible.

I can do all things through Christ who strengthens me.
-Philippians 4:13

Introduction

I wrote this book "No Ordinary Love" to share how God uses ordinary people like us, to bless however he wishes. For us, the blessing was in the form of an extraordinary love story. As time passed, people would often ask us, especially younger people, questions like "How long are we married? Or How long have you known each other?" Each time we share our story and how we met over 20 years ago, and married over a decade ago it amazes most of them.

Some would say we look too young to have known each other and to be married for that long and to that we say well we were young kids, 11 and 12 to be exact, when we fell in love at first sight. However, it wasn't all roses; we survived a long-distance friendship for 6 Years. That was way before social media, which made it even more challenging. We kept in touch by hand-written letters and long-distance land-line phone calls. But in the end, our love withstood the test of time and here we are today married for 11 years. We will celebrate our 12th year anniversary in June 2021, with our two beautiful children.

After years of repeating our love story and receiving the same astonished and amazed responses, regardless of the age, gender, or race of the person hearing our story, I knew we had a unique love story to share with the world. So I invite you into the heart of our pre-destined Caribbean romance.

Chapter 1

Growing up in Kingston, Jamaica

We both grew up during the 90s in Kingston, Jamaica. We lived in a tenement yard; tenement yards are quite common on the island. A tenement yard is a room, or house rented out by the owner, making us both byproducts of humble beginnings. This may have not afforded either of us luxurious lifestyles, but we are both certainly proud of where we come from. The great and famous Bob Marley also lived in a tenement yard once, and his reggae music is now heard world-wide.

Growing up in Kingston, in the heart of Jamaica, has not always been easy for us. His mom, as well as my parents, faced numerous hardships raising young children in the ghetto. Although it was not always easy; they did their best to provide for us, show us love, and instill good morals and values in us.

I moved to the community where he was born and raised when I was around five years old. While in basic school, I lived about four yards (houses) apart from him. We were neighbors and would later even live one yard (house) apart from each other.

We lived in the same community, so we both attended the same church, same schools, we had some of the same circle of friends, and we even went to the same aftercare. I recall following a friend to his yard to buy eggnog once. He would come to my yard for Bible study every week and also to buy things from a shop in my yard. We both passed each other maybe 1000 times over the years and still neither one of us had any recollection of seeing each other prior to meeting in 1998.

What's even more amazing when my mom and I would pass his yard, a lady standing at his gate would always smile and greet me pleasantly and I would smile back, not have an inkling that she would later become my mother-in-law and her son and I would soon fall in love.

Chapter 2

Migrating to the USA

In the fall of September 1996, life—as I knew it—forever changed. I departed the small island which I loved, to take residence in a strange land which, besides what I saw on TV, I knew very little of.

For the very first time in my life, I recall feeling sad. All I remember is that I did not want to leave my father, brother, and friends behind because they meant the world to me. Unfortunately, I did not have a choice in the matter; a decision was made without my input, and it was final. I was only nine years old at the time. I had so many awesome childhood memories; I wasn't prepared to leave them all behind. Among my favorite were when we played games like dolly house, dandy shandy, and rhythmic hand-clapping games, just to name a few. We laughed, we had lots of fun. Then, just like that, it was time to say goodbye to all I had ever known.

For how long? I did not know. My mother and I boarded our flights to America, and I can't imagine how she must've felt leaving behind her husband and one-year-old baby boy. One-good thing was that we were not here alone. I had lots of family awaiting us: grandma, grandpa, uncles, aunties, and cousins.

I attended school, but I did not make any friends at first. As a matter of fact, I was teased a lot about my hair styles (which were adorned with clips and bubbles aka barrettes), my drab clothing and my heavy Jamaican accent. My mom had to work very hard to provide for me. She was now living life much like a single mother. It was extremely challenging for the both of us to adjust to our new lives in the states. It differed greatly from what we both envisioned, but it was too late to go back.

So, we did our best to move forward and make the best of our situation. It was not easy, our beautiful family of four was now split in half. My mother's strength is far beyond my understanding. Looking back, I personally don't think I would have been able to do it, but she did it without complaining. She placed one foot in front of the other and never looked back. She wanted us to have a better life, so she and daddy both sacrificed and worked hard to provide a better future for us. When the people who love us make sacrifices for our benefit, we should never take them for granted. Instead we ought to express our gratitude every opportunity we get. After all, they didn't have to.

Chapter 3

Homesick

As time passed, I found myself homesick a whole lot. I missed my culture, the environment, my family, and my childhood friends. I suffered from culture shock in so many ways. For starters, I no longer wore school uniforms. Also, some of the American food differed from what I was accustomed to. However, I must admit, I thoroughly enjoyed eating pizza, something I don't recall eating back home. I missed eating bread fruit and picking genip of the tree and not to mention tamarind tree—my favorite, and Jamaican red apples—also another one of my favorites. I loved when mommy went to market every Saturday to buy them for me. I also missed waking up to the neighbors talking and playing their music and the atmosphere of living in the city and the roosters crowing that was our morning alarm clock.

It was utterly difficult, at first, adapting to the American way of living. I struggled to make friends in school, mainly because of my Jamaican accent and also because my mother could not afford trendy clothing—so the kids teased me. I also struggled to predominantly speak proper English instead of Patois so that people could understand me better. I honestly was not happy about that. I loved our broken English and speaking it made me feel proud of being a Jamaican. Don't get me wrong, it was not all bad. Florida was okay. The weather is similar to back home. Most of the tropical trees back home we have here also such as ackee, mangoes and sweet sop—you name it, most of them are here, yet still it was not home for me. Regardless how hard I tried to adapt, I felt like an outsider yearning to belong.

Another thing I especially enjoyed was the Thanksgiving Holiday tradition. We don't celebrate that holiday back in Jamaica, but it's become one of my favorite times of the year. Every year in November, my family and I look forward to seeing each other. We cook a mix of both Jamaican and American Food. Thinking back, turkey is something I never heard of before migrating. We laugh a lot and enjoy each other's company, same for Christmas time when grandma buys a real Christmas tree; I enjoy the fragrant aroma of pine. Grandma makes Jamaica's traditional sorrel drinks that she grows in her yard, which are the best if you ask me, and my auntie bakes the best traditional Jamaican Christmas cakes—so delicious; everyone enjoys themselves. These are some of the newer adopted traditions that I enjoy, especially spending quality time with family: my mommy, grandma, aunties, uncles, cousins and my great grandpa that I love so much he affectionately calls me TAE TAE.

Yet still, with all the fun I began having here, I would find myself reminiscing on the fun times I had back home, like visiting Saint Elizabeth Parish where daddy is from, visiting my grandma, cousins, aunties and uncles and not to mention my sister, "my twin", we are two years apart, but to us we are twins. Their accent is a little different from those of us from the city, and they talk a little fast for me, but I like to hear them speak. I love seeing the red dirt for miles and miles and just gazing at the scenic hills, mountains, and lands filled with bountiful crops—natural food for our body: yam, banana, pumpkin, you name it. Our family loaded up each trip with these, so much that my mom would share with our neighbors. I remember watching the farm animals during these trips, such as cows, pigs, and goats, and just feeling as if I was in a different world all together. It seemed far more tranquil and relaxed in comparison to the hustle and bustle of the city that I had grown accustomed to.

I missed spending quality family time together on the weekends such as visiting the zoo, or relaxing at the beach and eating fish and festival and my favorite bammy—oh so yummy, or the times we would window shop at the plaza, or have picnics at the park and always taking lots of pictures.

I also missed our Sunday tradition (when most shops and stores were closed). That was a day of worship and family time, when my friends and I attended church services in our Sunday best. Daddy cooked Sunday meals, like chicken with rice and peas, accompanied by a natural fruit juice that mommy made for supper. My friends and I would then ask our parents for money to buy ice cream and we would race to be the first to reach the ice cream man on his bicycle. Grape Nut was my favorite flavor and we then sat back, relaxed, laughed, and talked all while eating our ice creams. It felt as if life would always be this way.

Chapter 4

Returning to Jamaica

I was beyond thrilled in 1998, when my mom shared we would be visiting back home to see my father and brother. To be honest, it was long overdue. I could hardly contain myself. Oh, how much joy I felt! I had been homesick for two years and it had been way too long away from my home-sweet-home Jamaica. This pickney (child) missed the land of my birth. I missed authentic Jamaican food; such as jerk chicken, beef patty and even the sweety (candy); and my family and friends so much that words could not describe the happiness and joy I felt upon hearing this news. Me glad bag bus …. (extremely happy).

I remember I counted down the days that I would step foot on my island for the very first time since leaving. When the plane finally landed, it was the breath of fresh air my soul longed for. I was home again! I wanted to shout so the entire island could hear me JAMAICA MI DEH YAH (I am here)!

We reached home and were reunited and it felt oh so good. I wanted this moment to last forever. I knew in my heart that I did not want to return to America aka foreign again. Besides, there was so much catching up to do and a few weeks just wasn't enough time.

After a few days home with my family, I realized some things were exactly the same as I had left and some things had changed. For one, my two friends—they are sisters and also my BFF's—who lived in my yard, had moved across the street into their own home. The good thing was that it was still close enough for our friendship to remain the same. Thank goodness that did not change!

It surprised them that I had not changed one bit, and that my Jamaican accent (Tun up) was still on point. Mostly, things remained the familiar environment I had left behind two years prior. Bible study was still hosted in our yard, we still wore our Sunday best to church, the family tradition for Sunday remained the same and the best cooked meal for the week was still prepared on Sundays. Shops were mostly closed. On the weekends, my family and I spent a lot of quality time together; going to the plaza, visiting other family members, hanging out at the beaches, and seeing the different sites in Jamaica.

I still had lots of friends in my community who missed me. My mom and I would walk together across the street to my friend's house, the sister's veranda and catch up on everything we missed. We'd chat about what was new and what things were taking place in our community. I recall how good it felt to just laugh and have such good times. What I appreciated the most, simple as it may sound, was that as soon as I landed in Jamaica, I left my American accent on American soil. I spoke in my native tongue (Patois) all day, every day. My mom was not too pleased. She would repeatedly say, "you can speak proper English you know," but I couldn't help myself. Speaking patois filled my heart with gladness once again and I felt whole.

Chapter 5

Love at First Sight

Do you believe in love at first sight? This is how our not so ordinary story began over 20 years ago in Jamaica in 1998. I was 11 years old and he was 12, neither one of us was looking for love. We were just two kids. We knew nothing about love, but all that was about to change. I believe it was destined by God to put us together from our mother's wombs, that on this day and time we would lay eyes on each other and our lives would forever be changed. This was definitely not our plan, but the Lord's, and he would keep us together for a lifetime. This is truly a once in a lifetime kind of love. My only hope is that everyone experiences this love in their lifetime. It's a beautiful and wonderful gift from God.

    I was sitting on my friends' veranda, you know the sisters that moved across the street. We were chilling, laughing, and having a grand time, when all of a sudden I glanced at a boy walking by their house. I don't know why, but he seriously caught my attention. I was curious who he was. I began to question them "So who is that boy? What's his name? Where is he from?" I had never seen him before, so I thought he must have moved into our community after I migrated. They said "no girl, that's Sheldon, he has lived here all his life" and they pointed to his yard almost directly across the street from their home. I couldn't believe it. I began to wonder in my heart who he was and how it was possible that I had never seen him before. He was so handsome to me, so I think my friends noticed from my smile that I liked him. They knew from the start that I am the shyest person in the world. No lie I truly am.

As he passed by, one of the older sisters blurted "Kariesha likes you!" I ran into the house so fast that not even Usain Bolt, the fastest man in the world, who happens to be Jamaican born, could catch me. Once inside the living room, I heard him reply loudly, as if he wanted me to hear it, "tell her I like her too". I could not believe she said that. I don't even know this guy and I thought he was joking that he liked me. I really didn't even think he was serious, but us girls thought it was funny. We all giggled, especially me. I was laughing and smiling ear to ear, surprised but glad at the same time that she had really said that and that he even answered back.

I believe I fell in love that very moment—just like that—love at the very first sight of him. Looking back, I'm thankful to her for saying that I liked him because I don't know if I would be married today (due to my extreme shyness). So we are both grateful to her for what she did.

After that day, I was not sure if I would ever see him again, but my heart was secretly hoping I would. When I visited my friends again, while sitting on the veranda, I could see his yard across the street and I looked to see if he was there or passing by and sure enough he passed by one day and said, "hi" and I replied, "hi" back. Since he knew my friends, he would stop at their wall or gate from time to time, and we engaged in small talk. One day he brought me a picture of him when he was in about basic school (pre-K). He was even cuter back then. I asked him if I could keep the picture and he let me have it almost immediately after we met. I cannot explain it, but I knew from the first time we met that he would be my future husband.

Chapter 6

Adjusting to Life Abroad

After our trip back home, I believe mommy and I both decided in our hearts to try and adjust to making America our new home away from home. I now had a crush on a boy, but I kept it to myself. I told no one, besides I honestly did not know when I would be visiting Jamaica again. I made a few friends in middle school, luckily some were Jamaican, they made it easier to adjust to life here. We also found a church that we loved—a Jamaican Pastor and his family, they were so nice and gracious to us, we found comfort knowing we now had a church family.

Mommy continued to work hard as usual to provide a better future for us. She is my biggest inspiration. Never in my life have I met someone as strong as my mada (mother). We still had our share of struggles in America, especially being away from my father and my brother, but we kept in touch via handwritten letters and phone calls. I was surprised and super excited when a year later my mother suggested "let's go home and visit daddy and your brother again."

Chapter 7

Returning to Jamaica Again!

In December of 1999, my mother and I boarded a flight and headed back to Jamaica. We flew out a few weeks before the new millennium Y2K 2000 frenzy. Everywhere, everyone was nervous and anxious about the turn of the century—it was a big deal and some thought a digital meltdown would occur however in Jamaica we really thought Jesus' Second Coming was at hand. I am a daddy's girl from birth, so not having my father around really took a toll on me emotionally. It was especially difficult when I saw other kids with their fathers. I would get really sad. My father is a loving and kind, jovial man, although he is also a strict disciplinarian. I believe he's learned the true art of fatherhood. He works very hard to provide for us. You can always find daddy in the kitchen cooking up a storm. He absolutely loves to be in the kitchen. I know him for his great cooking skills: curry goat, oxtail, stew peas you name it he can cook it up. I also missed my little brother. We are eight years apart, so I feel like I have to protect him as his big sister. On this trip I was 12 years old—a preteen. I visited Canada to see my family in the summer. My aunties took me shopping and bought me a gold necklace and really nice trendy clothes so I felt superb, not to mention I finally felt cool.

I was now a young lady. My friends and I acted like typical pre-teens or teenagers who had crushes on boys, wore makeup, and did our nails. My parents were not happy about the makeup and nails, so I had to stop doing that for a while. No, they knew nothing about my crush at this point. I mentioned to mom that I had met my husband and she laughed at me for talking foolish. As a family, we spent a lot of quality time together. Each trip we visited family and friends. Mommy and I were on my friend's veranda hanging out one day, talking, laughing and catching up on all that we missed in a year, when suddenly I glanced up and guess who I saw?

Yes, my crush. He rode by quickly on his bicycle. What I didn't know until years later was that he was chilling with his friends when a friend told him I was back; the foreign girl a.k.a. American girl was back. I didn't consider myself a foreigner. I had only been away from Jamaica for two years, but that's beside the point. He did not believe his friend, so he rolled by to see for himself and sure enough it was me in living color. Our eyes met, but we could not say hi. My mom and other adults were there, so I tried to play it cool, but deep in my heart, I was beyond elated to see him once again.

Chapter 8

Puppy Love

The second trip around we got to know each other a little better. He would stop by my friend's (the sister's) yard to say hi and we would sometimes talk by their gate or wall. At church, we would see each other and I sometimes would walk over and say hi. The yard I lived in had a shop in the front. Sometimes I would spend time there with my friends, the sisters, and their mom who worked there. Years later, he shared with me how he would look for spare change just to stop by the shop to see me.

A mutual friend, one of our neighbors, would call me to the fence behind my house and Sheldon would be there when I went. I grew up with this particular neighbor, so if he called me my parents wouldn't think anything of it. But when he called me it really would be the two of us, my crush and I, talking by the fence. Somehow daddy found out one day after church and my dad approached the two of them and asked, "who is calling my daughter all the time to the fence?" my neighbor replied "me." Daddy warned him not to call me to the fence anymore.

A new set of siblings moved into our neighborhood. We quickly became friends, so I would walk next-door and sit on her veranda along with Sheldon and her brother. I was so shy at first I stayed on the step of the veranda and Sheldon had to call me up on the veranda to sit. All four of us sat there, he was too serious for me. He just looked at us as if we were acting too childish for him, but the three of us acted like fools. We played and acted silly and laughed and carried on. There was a kids treat at the park close by and I asked my mom's permission to go. We all went together with my BFF's (the sisters), and my new friend (the girl who moved to our community) and I remember he wore a khaki outfit, and I wore leopard print pants with a black top and black shoes. I remember thinking we all looked so good! We walked together and I was nervous that someone would see me walking with a boy and tell my parents. When we got there we all danced and had lots of fun and I felt some kind of way that he did not dance with me.

Years later he told me he thought I danced weird and that watching me dance was quite embarrassing for him. He is right though, I can't dance at all. I dance like I have two left feet. That was the beginning of our friendship. Until this day we still get a good laugh about this day, especially when he reenacts my dance moves at the kids treat, throwing his hands in the air all wild and shaking his body. I laugh at him looking silly saying I don't dance like that! But in reality, I do.

Chapter 9

First Kiss

One day I was sitting on my veranda and he was sitting on my friends veranda, (the siblings who recently moved in to our community) the brother and sister. We could both see each other from where we were sitting and I wanted to say hi, but I was just so shy and I had no idea how to approach him. So I decided to take some candy, a bag of gum I brought with me from America and offer him some. I walked over to him at the fence and said "do you want some bubblegum" and he said "yes," as he took them he asked me if he can have a chups (kiss)or peck. I thought about it for a minute and replied "yes." I first looked to my left and my right to see if anyone was coming or if anyone would see me because I'd be in big trouble and for the first time I kissed a boy and then I just walked right back to my veranda. I could not believe I actually kissed him. I did not sleep that entire night just thinking about it.

We decided to meet up at my yard under an ackee tree at night and we kissed two more times. We were not alone, our friends, (the brother and sister) were witnesses and watched for any adults who might pass by and see us. After our third kiss we both knew it was wrong to be sneaking around kissing behind our parents back. I had seen the movie Titanic and wanted us to be like Jack and Rose. It was Sheldon's idea to stop kissing. He did not want me to get in any trouble with my parents. He cared so much and I was surprised. I thought what a gentleman and we decided that we did not want our friendship to cross the line so we had to make boundaries.

We never discussed sex. It was just not something we talked about at our age. We were just two innocent kids in love. Not much changed after we kissed. I guess the kiss just sealed our friendship. We officially became boyfriend and girlfriend. Before I left he asked me for my number. I ran into my house looking nervously for a piece of paper to write on, quickly without thinking straight I ripped a piece of paper, the blank part that had no writings on it, out of the Bible and quickly ran back to him with it. We exchanged phone numbers. This was a big deal, remember now this was way before social media. We did not even have a cell phone; we would only use house phones. Daddy found the Bible with the ripped paper and he got upset. I could not believe I tore a paper out of the Bible! I don't think people think straight when they are in love. Forgive me Lord for tearing out of the The Bible (praying hands).

When I left Jamaica that winter year of 2000, I had no idea what the future held for us. I left Jamaica in love for the first time in my life. It felt so real. I felt like I had met my future husband.

Chapter 10

Long Distance Love

We both kept in touch as promised after we exchanged phone numbers. We could not afford calling cards and we were not old enough to work. So, a friend suggested we try collect calls. He warned me to keep it at one or two minutes maximum because of the charges. Well, he might as well have told me two hours, because once I start talking I can't stop.

I totally forgot about the charge's part until the phone bill came in, of course. My head started pounding and my heart raced a million miles per hour. It was too late. Mommy saw the phone bill and was furious! She found the only picture we had of each other and ripped it into tiny pieces. She told me I was too young to be in love or have a boyfriend, and both my parents agreed. She stated I would never go back to Jamaica again, and that it was in my best interest for things to be that way.

I cried for weeks. I was so angry at myself over everything. It was all my fault. My mom was already struggling to take care of me and make ends meet, and now I had added another expense.

Also mommy would no longer be taking trips back home to see her husband and son—all because of me.

I felt terrible about mommy and it crushed me that I would not see my boyfriend or friends ever again. We both saved our lunch money and brought calling cards and called each other occasionally. We also wrote letters. I eventually told him what my mom said, that I would never go to Jamaica again. We both agreed to keep in touch no matter what. When I was around 13, he wrote me a letter saying what age we would marry; he stated it would be at 20 and that we would have two kids—a boy and a girl, and that he was sure he didn't want anyone else to be his future wife and the mother of his children and that we would live in America. Almost everything he wrote to me or should I say predicted came to pass, the only difference was we actually married at 22 not 20 but still it was close enough.

I still have all of our love letters in a box and it's crazy reading them seeing how in love we were and also how bad our handwritings and spellings were back then.

Well, I was not sure about the future for us. I was in love, but we were both still so very young. Before we knew it one year turned into two and before we knew it six long years had gone by.

Chapter 11

Six Years Later

The first three years apart we were hopeful that maybe my parents would change their minds and allow me to visit my dad and brother again. However, when I was 15 years old daddy and my brother migrated. We were together again. One happy family. On the other hand, our friendship had grown apart and it became clear, now that daddy and my brother were here, that there was no chance of going back home. I think we both knew it, so during the last three years we became distant, and became busy with our own lives. Letters and calls were less frequent and we were teenagers now living our separate lives.

When I had some down time my mind often drifted and I wondered if he had a girlfriend, but I never mustered up the courage to ask him. Maybe, the truth was that I did not want to know the answer. I, on the other hand, had no boyfriend. I am a Christian and my faith in God is super important to me, so I kept far away from boys. I had some opportunities to talk to boys, but I turned them down. My heart was on my first love. I did not want to pretend to be in love with someone else and risk breaking someone's heart.

When I turned 18—a few weeks after graduating high school—that summer in 2005 (right before starting nursing school), I asked my parents if I could visit my friends in Jamaica and also him. Surprisingly, my parents agreed, but it was under one condition—my mom basically had to be my chaperone on this trip. Out of respect for them, I agreed.

We stayed at a family friends home in another city. By this time he had started trade school to study carpentry. He attended a school in the city where I was staying, so after school one day he decided to meet me. My mom's friend and I waited for him on the street sidewalk. We could see him from a distance walking closer and closer to us. I suddenly became so nervous I thought I would pass out. The closer he got the more I realized his features had changed. He looked far different from the 12 year old boy I met many moons ago. He was a man now. Finally, after what seemed like an eternity we reached the house. The whole time I couldn't stop looking at him. I kept thinking to myself we don't seem to have the same connection or love we once had. I wondered why something just did not feel right. I even mentioned it to my mom's friend. We talked and chatted a bit, he could not stay long. He had to take a bus back home so he came over on the weekend to visit. My mom gave us some raw peanuts to shell. We sat on the couch and as soon as she left the room we kissed and laughed and talked. My mom came back some minutes later and asked what we were doing since it looked like we had only shelled five of the peanuts. We smiled and started shelling some more.

My mom and I visited our friends, the sisters. We sat on the veranda (porch) and it reminded me so much of the good old times. We laughed, we talked, and had so much to catch up on. He came over and asked my mom permission to show me his house and introduce me to his family. She agreed so I walked with him across the street. After all this time, I found myself still so nervous to be walking with a boy.

He introduced me to his neighbors as his girlfriend. Before we entered his house, he proudly showed me the pigeons he was raising. I had brought with me the movie *The Notebook* so we could watch it together. I told him he would enjoy the movie since it was similar to our story. We didn't actually get to watch it. We sat on the bed and kissed. I was so nervous. This was our first time ever alone. Even in our younger days, kissing under the ackee tree, our friends watched us, so it was weird to me, but he was a perfect gentleman as always. He knew I was a Christian and my heart's desire was to save sex for marriage, so no hanky-panky occured. Shortly afterwards, his mom came home from work as well as his older brother, so I was officially introduced to them. Although I had seen his mom, as a little girl passing by and I recall seeing his brother before, I was now being formally introduced to them. On the weekend we decided to visit Emancipation Park, and my mom, of course, chaperoned me. She sat with us on the very same bench. It was awkward to say the least.

I left this trip feeling confused about us and our future. I was troubled by so many unanswered questions. I was happy to see my friends again, but as far as our friendship it seemed uncertain. I came back home feeling unsure. So I did the only thing I knew to do when I felt this way—pray. When I was done, I found a piece of paper I previously wrote on, it was a list of good qualities that I wanted in a husband. I placed it in my Bible and I prayed again and asked God to guide and show me and lead me in the right direction of whether I should remain in this long distance friendship or if I should just get on with my life. I kept myself distracted and busy with nursing school and work. God works in mysterious ways. When I least expected it and in the most unseemly way, God showed me exactly what to do.

Chapter 12

Grandpa's Funeral

Almost two years passed since my last trip to Jamaica in 2005 with my mom. When I returned from that trip I had many unanswered questions. It felt as if our friendship was at a standstill. I did not know if I should stay or move on. I kept praying about it. In my heart, I knew God's promise for us. I knew since age 11 he was my husband, but what I could not understand was why the love and connection seemed to be no longer there. That was crystal clear from my last trip back home. It all felt so vague.

When my father told me my grandpa died and asked if I would like to go with him, what he said next shocked me. He said I could invite my friend, the boy I was talking to. I could not believe my ears. I don't know how he knew about us. I never discussed us with daddy. However, he was once a young man himself. It was December 2007 and it just so happened to be winter break from nursing school. Talk about God's perfect timing!

I called Sheldon and told him I was coming, only this time I would not be in the city where we are from. Daddy made it clear we were not visiting the city, so he had to come visit me this time. He told me he could only get the weekend off. He graduated trade school and was now working as a full-time carpenter.

He arrived late Friday night and explained how he almost got lost and was about to turn back, when they decided to stop one last time to ask for directions. They stopped at a shop where he asked the lady if she knew of an old man who died. I had told him grandpa's pet name and she pointed next-door.

My family was setting up a celebration of life before his funeral. I was getting my hair braided when I looked up and he touched my hand. It was like sparks flew everywhere—no more like fireworks, he was looking oh so fine. I blushed the entire time I was getting my hair done. Once again, I couldn't stop looking at him. When I finished my hair, we went somewhere quiet, away from the crowded noise, and talked. Daddy did not chaperone us; he trusted the both of us. Besides, I was now twenty years old and an adult. Yet it surprised me still, being that he was so strict raising me. We talked the entire night. We had a lot of catching up and reminiscing to do.

The following day, we attended grandpa's funeral. We both looked so nice and well-dressed. We sat in the church together. I read a scripture at the funeral service. After the funeral I told him I had something to share with him; I had an older sister, by my dad, before he met my mom, and she lived here in the countryside. We walked to her house and as soon as he saw her he blurted "yes, that's your dad's twin for sure."

I also introduced him to the rest of my family and they all liked him. I was overjoyed to see my family from Canada in Jamaica again, although it was under sad circumstances. We took walks and we literally spent every minute together. Sunday was the last day. The lovely weekend came to an abrupt end. It was time for him to go back to work. He held my hand gently—I remember thinking his hands were so handsome—and he proceeded to tell me how he wanted me to be his wife as soon as I graduated from nursing school. He said he would work hard to save his money and take me to a fancy jewelry shop in the plaza where I could pick out any ring I wanted. That was sweet music to my ears.

After having spent the weekend together I got to know his heart. He was a responsible, hard-working, loving, and caring young man, far ahead of his years, and he had far exceeded all the qualities I had written down for my future husband. I knew he was the one to be my forever. I knew from the first day we met and now I have no doubt. There was just one slight problem. I still could not look in his eyes. I was so shy, he held my hand and gently asked how I could be his future wife when I wouldn't look into his eyes. It took about five minutes of him convincing me to look in his eyes. When I finally did, I could not stop staring at him. It was like I could see right through the man. I could see my future, our future kids, everything.

Funny how we were taking selfies with my new camera, before we even knew what a selfie was. Although this trip was due to a sad occasion, I thank daddy for inviting him to my grandpa's funeral. Sometimes I don't understand God and what he does. I try not to question the creator of everything. All I know is I left that trip and we were falling in love more than I ever felt before. I felt like my life had purpose. We had been through a lot together, (being apart was utterly difficult) and our friendship survived it all. Love conquered in the end and I was looking forward to being his wife more than anything.

Chapter 13

Our Engagement

After I returned from my grandpa's funeral, he called and said he had something to tell me. He started by saying how much he wanted me to be his wife. He then went on to say that he first needed to be honest with me before we got engaged. He shared he was at work talking to a Christian coworker about us, and the guy advised him to be completely honest. He confessed that he was not a virgin, that he made some mistakes, had a few girlfriends, and that he got peer-pressured into seeing other people. He explained that every time he hung around his friends they would ask where his girl was, and that when he would reply "America" they would say "America man? You live in Jamaica!" The teasing intensified when I returned to Jamaica with my mom, when he invited me to his house to introduce me to his family. When I left the yard they asked him did we do it, when he said "no" that's when the laughing and teasing got worse, he naturally wanted to fit in and be a part of what everyone was doing. So he said he wanted to tell me at grandpa's funeral, but he just did not have the courage to do so. He said after the funeral he stopped talking to the girls and even told them about me. That he would not continue to live a lie and living that kind of lifestyle. He knew he wanted to be with just one woman; his wife and he wanted it to be me, he asked if I could forgive him.

I was so shocked by what happened and what I heard that I hung up the phone on him. I needed time to clear my thoughts and called him back later, that evening. We talked about it. I told him I would think about it. I was just devastated. My heart was broken. The perfect love story that I wanted us to have had just ended. I wrestled with all kinds of thoughts. Here I was saving my body for this man, for when we get married, and now this? I wanted to tell him I too got peer-pressured in school, but I never gave in. I waited! I'm still waiting! I just could not comprehend why he could not do the same. I reflected over all the years and 100 memories flashed before me. One in particular was the trip I took with my mom after high school graduation. Now I see and understand why there was a disconnection between us. This was the puzzle solved. He had not been honest and faithful. Believe it or not, the moment I saw him I just knew in my heart. The Lord always reveals things to me, but sometimes I just ignore it.

Should I forgive him? I thought long and hard about it. I wanted to confide in my mom or a friend for directions on what to do, but I instantly felt the Lord in my heart say no, that it would only bring confusion. One will say stop talking to him and move on and one will say stay with him. So I prayed and prayed about it. I eventually called him and said that I forgave him. Not because he was a young man, a teenager who gave in to peer pressure, but because we all make mistakes, even myself. I too had to ask the Lord for forgiveness. When I prayed, I felt in my heart that he was sorry and sincere. I told him never, and I meant never to be unfaithful again.

Looking back on over a decade of being married, it was the best decision of my life. He has been faithful to me all these years. He confided in me that he made a promise to God that if he ever cheated or broke my heart, that God could punish him, because I have been a good friend and wife to him over the years. He proudly tells his friends and other young men that he is faithful to me all these years in our marriage, he encourages friends and young men to do the same in their relationships.

Also, after our heart-to-heart talk over the phone, we both started a new page, and we moved on.

A year later, I graduated from nursing school. It was December 2008. Exactly one year after grandpa's funeral. I called him up with excitement in my voice. I remembered his words to me at grandpa's funeral. He said as soon as you graduate nursing school I will work hard to save my money and engage you. I was so happy that he kept his word. So, I told my parents. Yes, I was still living at home, working, and going to nursing school. My parents said it was my decision. I was 21 and an adult. So I boarded my flight to Kingston, Jamaica to get engaged.

By this time he moved out of the community where we both grew up and lived in another community in Kingston. For the very first time, we both went on an official date with no adults around. We visited the zoo, the famous Devon house to enjoy the most delicious ice cream in all of Jamaica. He then took me to get pampered and get my hair and nails done—all paid for by him. He introduced me to his extended family. They welcomed me into the family and they took me to the famous Dunn's River Falls. It was my first time there and it was so much fun. We also visited Saint Elizabeth to visit my sister and family. We went on some more dates in the country to the famous Lover's Leap. It was so beautiful, the view over the cliff was breathtaking, the ocean and clouds met together— it was a sight to see. They named Lover's Leap after two slave lovers from the 18th century, and legend has it, that their master took a liking to the girl and in a bid to keep her for himself, he arranged for her lover to be sold to another estate. They ran away to avoid being separated, but they were chased to the edge of a large, deep cliff and jumped off together, rather than being forced to be separated.

We also visited treasure beach. We were having the time of our lives. He then took me to a really nice jewelry store as promised. I was so shy and nervous that I could not pick out a ring, so the clerk helped me to decide on one. He proposed and I said "yes." I was just so excited. I was 21 and a young bride to be. I was looking forward to becoming Mrs. Topping.

Chapter 14

Our Wedding

In June 2009 we said our vows before about 40 witnesses. I wish I could say that it was all I prayed for and had envisioned since we first met (at 11 years old), but it was not. I had a mixture of emotional feelings of overjoyed to finally getting married to my childhood sweetheart and also my heartaches with disappointments and distress on my wedding day, but I held my composure and smiled through my storm. After all this was my day. It's far too personal and hurtful to write about, but I will say I have chosen to forgive. In life, we have choices either to live with fear and regrets or choose to not let anything or anyone steal our joy and triumph over our situations —no matter what! I choose both joy and triumph.

Nehemiah 8:10 The Joy of the Lord is my Strength.

I'm a child of the most high God and I am stronger than I think I am. The Lord was with us and he approved our union. Satan himself cannot destroy what God joins together. My wedding day was not all bad. It was sheer joy seeing the sisters—my Bff's, along with many of our childhood friends, my parents, our family friend—the lady whose house we stayed at on our trip to Jamaica with my mom, my brother and grandmother, and his family in attendance, who all came to support us.

I felt like a queen when daddy walked me down the aisle, in my beautiful white dress and white shoes, long white veil, and borrowed white gloves. Everything had sparkles and bling—lots of bling-bling. My hair and nails were styled beautifully. I wore a lovely tiara with more bling. We looked gorgeous, if I must say so myself (wink), and there was my handsome earthly king waiting for me, dressed in all white like me. We said our vows, before God and man, and that day we became one. I chose the colors red and white; my bridesmaids wore red dresses. The pastor that married us was so nice. He prayed blessings upon us; that we would be prosperous, fruitful, and multiply. I felt every word of his prayer and I knew God had already blessed us and that we would multiply in due time. I felt a profound peace like no other, during and after the pastor's prayer. It felt as if God gave me a confirmation in my heart that all would be well. We sang the song, Great is thy Faithfulness. The reception was outdoors, it was well decorated and the cake table looked amazing. A beautiful decorated 3-tier white cake, with red roses on top, and red waterfalls completed the decor; and it actually tasted even better than it looked.

I invited my Pastor and his wife and he gave a nice speech and I was so shy when we had our dance that I could not look at anyone. I put my head on his chest the whole time. We had waiters and waitresses dressed in black and white attire who served the food. More people came to the reception. My favorite part was being serenaded by a group of young men in a singing group. They sang Kenny Rogers Write Your Name. It was my first time hearing that song, but it was lovely. I listened to every word of this song. After our wedding we went to the Pegasus hotel. I chose that hotel. My parents gave us $500 us dollars for our wedding gift so we used it for our hotel stay. We had a nice view from our room of the city and the room was appropriately decorated with fruits, wine, red roses, and lovely decorated towels on the bed. It was absolutely beautiful.

That night we became Mr. and Mrs. for the very first time. We talked about our future and I was hoping for a honeymoon baby. On our honeymoon I felt like the Lord said "no, it's not the right time." We had an all you can eat authentic Jamaican food buffet, in the morning, for breakfast. It was scrumptious and included ackee and saltfish, Jamaica's national dish and my favorite meal served with fried dumplings .

Emancipation Park was across the street. Yes, the same park we sat on the bench with mommy on that trip years ago. We took walks there during the day and night. We had a wonderful time, just the two of us, celebrating God's will in bringing this union together. I wish that moment could pause forever, we were young and in love and married. God is good all the time and I'm grateful to still be married to my best friend for a decade and to be in each other's lives for over 20 years. I am looking forward to renewing our vows one day, so that I can have the wedding of my dreams. The one i envisioned many years ago as a child, but I know now nothing happens before God's time.

Chapter 15

Family of Three

A little over a year after we got married, my husband migrated from Jamaica to join me here in the states. We did not waste any time. We started a family right away. We had all kinds of emotions about the news of my pregnancy ranging from joy to excitement to uncertainty. We were not financially prepared and so we were, at times, worried about the future for the three of us. He accompanied me to almost every ultrasound and I was so nervous to know the gender of our baby. Oh, how I hoped for a girl and he of course hoped for a boy. How surprised I was when the doctor announced it was a boy. At first, I was a bit disappointed. I really wanted a girl, but both he and the doctor reminded me I should be grateful and happy that I was having a healthy baby. So, I dried my tears and accepted what God gave me. I instantly felt so much joy that God blessed my womb with a child. Before he was born, we prayed over him in my belly that blessings would be over his life. We also prayed many prayers of gratitude for being chosen as his parents. The very first time we laid eyes on him we both instantly fell in love and we vowed to be the best parents we could be and work hard to give him a better future. Today, he is one of my greatest joys. God always knows best!

We lived with my parents at the time, so as soon as he could he got a minimum-wage job, which did not pay much, but it was a start. I had to stop work a few months into my pregnancy. We were looking for a place to rent, because our budget was $500 and even almost 10 years ago that was pretty much nearly impossible. Everywhere we looked and asked, the minimum was around $800. One day we were driving around town and I felt the Lord telling me to pull over to a plaza. There was a real estate business and I asked my husband to go inside with me, but honestly I was scared to ask, due to our budget, if they had any rooms for rent in our budget, and to our surprise she said "yes." We followed the Realtor. There was a house in the front of the yard and a tiny house in the back about 400 square feet. Not much larger than a two car garage. We agreed to it right away. It had everything we wanted, was within our budget, and we couldn't be picky in our situation. It had a bedroom, bathroom, a tiny kitchen and living room space, so we moved in right away. I believe this was only the beginning of miracles, because this truly was a miracle from God that we desperately needed.

We settled into our new home. My husband worked nights. It was hard for me at first, especially being pregnant, being alone at night in a new home and community. Eventually I got used to it and trusted God to protect both me and the growing baby inside of me. Before I knew, it was time for our baby shower, which by the way, turned out to be more like a family reunion.

Some of My husband's family flew in, some came from far away to support our baby shower, some family he met for the very first time. My family and friends showed up. It was held at a park in front of a lovely waterfall, with well-decorated arrangements, and a beautiful cake. It was just amazing, we both felt so blessed by all the love and gifts we received for our little guy. Before we knew it, our 6 pounds, bouncing baby boy arrived in August 2011. Hubby was right by my side through it all. The joy we felt that day no words can describe. It was a feeling we will never forget as long as we live. We both created another human being in our flesh and blood. Our son is his daddy's twin for sure. We were overjoyed that God blessed my womb to bring forth this wonderful child. So here we were now a family of three.

      We experienced quite a bit of financial difficulty, at first. I drove an old jalopy, I believe it was a 92 Toyota Tercel, 2 door and the AC did not work. We had to save up to get it fixed, but God was with us. We never complained or went around having a pity party despite our many financial difficulties, we were a team and were in it to win it. When my baby was about three months old, I returned to work and we both worked very hard. We had lots of big dreams for our baby boy and we knew the only way to accomplish them was through the sweat of our brows. We knew we had to work hard and that's exactly what we did. Some days we would not see or spend time with each other, but we both knew our hard work would not go in vain.

Chapter 16

Dream Big

Our baby boy was two years old and quickly outgrew our, tiny home. So I prayed hard to the Lord for a bigger place. We went back to the same plaza and Realtor we explained we were seeking a two bedroom for rent. By this time, my hubby and I had found better-paying jobs. He showed us a place, but right away hubby did not like it. He didn't like the neighborhood and worried about me working the night shift as a nurse and coming home late. He wanted me to have a safe place. The Realtor overheard my hubby and I reasoning about the place. The Realtor asked if we ever considered buying a house. Yes, we had actually thought about it, but never thought being a homeowner was possible at the time for us. I mean, we were not making significant income. He said for us to gather our job, bank, and other paperwork and he got on it right away and to our surprise he said we qualified for home ownership. Our hearts were pounding. We could not believe it. We eventually went house hunting. The first house was in our budget, but it had a pond in the back and no fence, that was a big no-no for our toddler. Also, hubby wanted a two car garage, but it had only one. All I wanted was a backyard. Our Realtor said he had another home close by, it's a little over our budget, in a gated community, and he thought we would like it. We went and on our first look we said yes immediately. It was a nice two-story, two-car garage, with a nice backyard. It had everything and more than what we prayed for or wanted. On December 26th, a day after Christmas, we received keys to our new home. It was a belated Christmas gift from our heavenly father, that was the best belated Christmas gift of our lives. We were elated that all our hard work was finally paying off. Our baby boy had more than enough space to run around and it felt like a mansion to us at first, because we were so used to living in that tiny space—a size just a little bigger than our garage—for three long years. We were so happy our son had his own room that we adopted a puppy from the pound, so he had him to play with.

    Honestly, looking back on this, for me, is by far one of the happiest days of my entire life. Things became a lot brighter for us, but we were not rich, we still had to continue working hard in order to pay our mortgage and provide for our son. We knew that with hard work and determination we could accomplish anything in life. Nothing was too big or small. Pray and seek the Lord always and he will direct your path. He did it for us, he can do it for you. Mommy always says " if yuh want good yuh nose haffi run " in other words whatever you want to achieve in life you have to be willing to work hard and persevere.

Chapter 17

My Queen

To say I was overjoyed when I found out I was pregnant in 2015 is an understatement. I prayed for her like I never prayed for anything in my life. We planned for her right down to the T, and we got pregnant right away. Everything about this pregnancy went as planned. I always dreamed about having a girl from a young age. My mom always dressed me with frills, and did my hair, and did all the girly things, and I wanted to experience the same thing one day. So it thrilled me when my OB/GYN announced we were having a girl. I made her check like two extra times. I wanted to make sure 100% that I had no surprises at the time of delivery. Sure enough, as I expected, my queen arrived. I always refer to her as a queen, she is a queen to me.

I had to stop working as a nurse when I was around six months pregnant. I kept feeling weak and dizzy for a few weeks especially at work I kept ignoring the signs I thought each pregnancy is different and they were normal pregnancy symptoms after all I was working long 12-hour shifts so I figured that's the reason why my mom convinced me to go to my Dr. I went to the ER they told me I was anemic he called my ob-gyn and they agreed on the best treatment for me, they prescribed iron tablets. The doctor asked me if I was taking prenatal vitamins, I replied yes, he asked if they had iron in it, I said I think so. When I got home I checked and this particular prenatal vitamins did not have iron. I took the prescribed iron tablet and I felt better a few days after that ordeal. I stayed home during the rest of my pregnancy to recuperate besides I was hardly able to walk at this point (without being short of breath). How could I complete 12-hour shifts like that? Little did I know this was just the beginning of what was to come next.

Once I stopped working, things became a little difficult financially, but God kept us and we got through the pregnancy. We also had a nice baby shower. Once again, family and friends showed their love and support for us. I planned things down to the T, but her delivery was far from what we planned for. I had scheduled a C-section with my doctor, which I requested because of her size (she was over eight pounds, closer to nine) and also because I had difficulty delivering our son naturally and he was only 6 pounds. Our baby girl arrived a day earlier than expected, and hubby was at work and could not make it. He requested the day of the scheduled C-section off from work, but our baby girl came the day before—surprise! It greatly disappointed me that he couldn't make it. My dad drove me to the hospital, and a friend stayed with me until she was born. When I heard my baby's first cry, I could not help it, tears of joy streamed down my face. I thanked God for both answering my prayer for a daughter and for sparing my life during surgery. I have my African Queen Keke.

Chapter 18

For Better or Worse

Almost immediately after giving birth, I noticed the swelling in my body getting progressively worse, especially in my legs. They hurt a lot. My complexion also got a lot darker. I just did not feel or look well. I was staying with my parents for a few days while I recovered from my C-section. My husband had to work and I needed help with the baby—and with our son still in school, we really needed the help.

I noticed I was not feeling any better, but I ignored the signs. I thought I only had a few days left before my next OB/GYN check up. So I waited for my OB/GYN visit, but for some reason that morning I woke up with a terrible headache. I did not know it then, but that headache would save my life. My husband took me to the OB/GYN doctor. They checked my blood pressure and it was high, the doctor asked if I had a history of high blood pressure to which I replied, 'no, never." I also told her about my swelling. She was about to write me a prescription and send me home, but she asked me one question that

I believe saved my life, she said by the way have you had any headaches recently? I said "yes, a matter of fact i had a migraine earlier today" she quickly wrote on a piece of paper and handed it to me. She said "you need to be in ICU right now" I said, "now?" She explained that my life depended on it. I asked if I could go home and pack and by the look on her face I knew it was too serious to play with. She said "no time to pack. Go now, bye!" Thankfully, the hospital was right next to her office. She said, "I believe you have all the signs and symptoms of postpartum pre-eclampsia and it can be very dangerous and potentially deadly." I had studied about its dangers in nursing school, but I never thought in a million years this would happen to me. So, I went to the hospital and gave them the doctor's note, but the ICU was full. No bed was available and I spent the night in the ER.

    I developed a fever that night and the next morning they sent me to the ICU. I had to get IV meds. They told me it was to save my life, but that it also could cause seizures. I prayed to God to save my life. I was so scared. Emotionally, I was a mess. I cried all day for my baby. I begged the nurse to let me see her just one more time, just in case I did not make it out of the hospital alive, but they told me the hospital was no place for a baby. Especially the ICU. One of the side effects of the IV's was a migraine headache. It was so bad I told them to do a scan of my head. It was so lonely in the hospital. My husband had to work and take care of the two kids. My parents and a friend helped out. I prayed that I would step out of this hospital alive. I was really scared for my life. I also developed a breast infection. I guess from not breast-feeding or expressing the milk. I had to be on antibiotics for it. I was also prescribed blood pressure pills. I will never forget a nurse who came to me and told me, after I think it was 20+ years working as a nurse, to count myself a blessed lady because she had never had an ICU patient who could talk, walk, get out of bed and eat all at the same time. It was then that I looked around me and realized she was right. That none of these patients were able to do what I was doing. Sadly, most of them were on life-support with tubes down their throats. In fact, most of them had tubes placed all over them to help keep them alive. When I looked around she was so right. I was the only one who was well enough to do all these things. It was then I began to have a heart of gratitude and praise all at the same time. I was fighting for my life all right, but I was able to walk, to use all my senses, and everything was working. Eventually she told me to stay in bed and that I had to have compression on both my legs. I also had to get injections to prevent blood clots everyday and had IV's in both arms. The next day I went to a step down unit and was out of the ICU. I was happy I was getting better and excited to get discharged to go home. I spent three days total in the hospital and lost 30 pounds during my stay. How do I know I lost so much weight? The nurse weighed me in the hospital bed, also a dress I wore prior to the hospital now just hangs loosely on me, so much so I thought it was a different dress—it was an unbelievable sight to see . I was so thankful to God when I got out of the hospital. I wanted to kiss the ground that day as the man pushed me in a wheelchair. Three days in the hospital felt like a lifetime.

    I returned to work five months later. Things seemed to be going fine until around October 2017. A year and half later after I had my baby, I started feeling ill, not like myself. I began having back pains and the pain kept getting worse. I requested some time off from my job and they granted me three months off. After I had my baby, and the ICU ordeal, I never went back to work full-time. I did Per-Diem work, so my job encouraged me to take the time off to nurse my health.

    Doctor after doctor visit it seemed like my health was

getting worse. The pain in my back intensified. It became unbearable to the point I could no longer do the things I took for granted, like driving, ushering at church, cleaning my home, and bathing my daughter. All these once simple things became difficult tasks. I had to take pain meds just to be able to keep up with everything. My husband had to help me out a lot. The doctor told me I had several kidney stones, but she still was not sure what was causing the severe back aches. She did blood work, but advised me to refrain from administering the pain meds I was taking almost daily, because she was concerned that although the meds might alleviate the pain, they could also cause damage to my liver. She suggested another pain med, but I did not know what to do at that point. I was scared to take anything for pain. Each day grew worse than the day before. Most of my days were filled with pain. I would fold myself into a fetal position and cry most of the time. My kids saw me crying every single day. Also, my three months were up and I could not return to work. I had to tell them I was not getting any better. Our financial struggles began to get worse. Not only did we have to cover the cost of each doctor visit, but diagnostic tests and prescriptions began to add up quickly.

 I had a mountain stack of hospital bills. Things took a toll on my marriage. It was difficult for my husband to keep up with my challenging health, and all the bills, plus our mortgage. I was frustrated being sick all the time. He was taking the brunt of all the burdens and also having to help me out with the housework and on top of it go to work and do his job. It had become unbearable for both of us. At one point things were so bad, that we even mentioned divorce. We just did not know a way out of everything we were experiencing in our marriage.

 Emotionally, it was hard on me. I was perpetually sad throughout this time. I just did not understand why I was going through this as a young woman and mother of young children that needed me, who had my whole life and future ahead of me, I was now unemployed and feeling very sick. Very few people knew what I was going through. I'd always kept a smile on my face and as if things were not already bad enough, my health continued to worsen. Not only was I suffering from severe backaches, but now my side was experiencing excruciating pain that would, at times, almost knock me to my knees. I was miserable to say the least and the pain meds were no longer helping. My health took a toll and got worse. I admitted myself to the ER. They did a scan and told me I needed to do surgery ASAP. I could not believe it. All the memories of my C-section and ICU experience began to flood my mind.

I underwent abdominal surgery in 2019. I was grateful for the surgery, but I still had one prayer request because that same backache was by far worse at times than the side pain that I just had surgery for. At the end of 2018, New Year's eve night at church, I prayed to God to heal my back for the new year 2019 and to transform my life.

I kept praying and trusting God to work a miracle. I then met a friend in my church and we became close. I was not sure if I should confide in her all that I was going through. But I felt that she could be trusted, I told her about my marriage and she prayed. As soon as she prayed, she got a vision from God right away that not only would we not divorce, but that God would use our marriage as a ministry to help others. Who knows maybe this book is the start of that ministry. After all it's our testimony to help others.

A few months later, my marriage got completely restored. A few weeks after, I felt the Lord nudging me to give up my career as a nurse. I know it's shocking to some people, but I did just that and I felt free obeying the Lord. He did that for a purpose and for my destiny and as soon as I did it, the idea for this book was born. I also became an aspiring entrepreneur. Wait, it gets better... My same church friend, the one who prayed for my marriage; one day I drove to meet her desperate for healing, she prayed for my back and with her faith and mine, my back was healed. I didn't even realize it was healed. I was talking to my mom one day and she said to me I have not heard you cry for your back in a while." I said with excitement, "you know mommy you're right!" It'd been a few weeks, so I called my church sister right away. I said,

"I think I got healed!" She said don't simply think so, believe and trust God that you are healed. I know I got healed and that was it, my life got better and my story gets better.

I was feeling so good, I prayed for a job and God opened one with the perfect schedule for my family. Thank you Jesus! All the trials and tribulations that I went through these past few years, I wouldn't wish on my worst enemy, if I had one. It was pure hell on earth, but my favorite scriptures gave me strength.

And he said to me My Grace is
sufficient for you, for my strength is made
perfect in your weakness. -2 Corinthians 12 :9-10

I'm so glad we never got a divorce! That would have caused us to throw away 10+ years of marriage, and our 20 year friendship. I'm so happy my husband stuck to his vows to me. For better or worse, sickness or health, rich or poor, we certainly had our share of health crises in our marriage and financial struggles, but we are still together as a family. It did not break us, it made us stronger. All may not be perfect, but it is a testament for people, that no matter what your circumstance, bring it before the Lord and he will fight your battles. Our lives are not perfect neither is our marriage. My health is not 100% either, but we are blessed. Our marriage and children are blessed. I didn't think we would make it while I was going through my suffering. I felt like there was no way out, no light, or breakthrough, but I trusted God.

I never stopped praying for a miracle for my marriage, our children, and our finances. Mommy always says we never stop working till the day we die. So, for the things that are important to you, don't give up, keep working at it, keep praying and have faith. I am a living testimony.

Chapter 19

Love Letter to my Best Friend

I feel so blessed to be able to call you, my hubby and my best friend. However, we both know that it didn't start out that way; it happened gradually over the years. For me, I would say it blossomed at grandpa's funeral from our first heart-to-heart talk. That memory is one that is so near and dear to my heart. It was then that I realized, for the first time, that you are a man who is nurturing, loving, and protective of me. That you have my best interest at heart—always. I have had little-to-no success with friendships over the years, and as my hubby and a witness to that you often feel bad for me. I would try my best to be a loving and genuine friend, but in the end people took my kindness for weakness. I was also timid and people took advantage of that. People mistook me, often leaving me in an emotional wreck wrestling with trust issues. I even brought some of the issues over into my marriage. Forgive me, for those things. I have learned to trust in your love for me.

As my husband you've worked hard to regain my trust from what had happened and you reassure me how you would not leave nor forsake me. I've witnessed you take our marriage vows seriously and stand by me, no matter what. Not only have you spoken these nice words, but you prove it daily; by your actions, time and time again. Through sickness and being unemployed for years, you stood right by my side. For better or worse, you proceeded to take good care of me and the children. I do not know what or where I would be without you!

I love you to the moon, sun, stars and back. Cheers to 20-plus years of friendship and 11 years of marriage. I'm so glad that God brought you into my life. He knew I would need a friendship like yours to keep me going when I am weak and need a shoulder to cry on. God knows best always!

Nuff love to you my hunny bunny my Jamaican king from your Jamaican Queen with love.

Chapter 20

My Prayer for You

Looking over the past 23 years, since I met and fell in love with my husband at age 11, my childhood sweetheart, I can totally say, I am blessed beyond measure. People say they search their whole lives to experience true love like ours. I have that with my husband Sheldon. We had our share of ups and downs, trials and tribulations, but through it all love prevailed. Love really does conquer all, as the Bible says.

My parents played a crucial role in it all. Although I was angry when they found out about our friendship and separated us; I did not understand it then—as a child. However, now that I have an almost 10-year-old son, it all makes sense and I agree with their decision. They did the best thing for us by not condoning two kids to fall in love and do as they pleased. I did not write this book to say it's OK for children to fall in love, but as a testament of our lives. It just happened to be that we fell in love while we were young and it has lasted over two decades.

I wrote this book to hopefully inspire everyone, who

reads our story, both young and old, to believe in love. Love does exist!

Also, marriage, children, and family are sacred and beautiful gifts from God that should be cherished, loved , and nurtured. I hope after reading this book, it inspires you to love more, hope more and have more faith.

> *"For I know the plans I have for you"*
> *declares the Lord,*
> *"plans to prosper you and not to harm you*
> *plans to give you hope and a future.*
>
> *-Jeremiah 29: 11*

I pray that everyone who reads my book will be encouraged and blessed whether you are married, single, or engaged that God has designed and created someone uniquely special, on this earth, just for you.

Some people, like myself and my hubby, have been fortunate and blessed to find that someone special right away. For others, it takes time. However, no matter how long you've waited, be patient, pray, and the Lord will lead you. Don't make the mistakes that many make by seeking and dating those who don't have marriage in mind. This doesn't mean don't be selective, but date with the purpose of being united in Holy Matrimony.

PRAYER FOR EXTRAORDINARY LOVE:

Heavenly Father, You are most omnipotent. I believe in your plans for my life and I now release all fear, resistance, and rebellion holding me back from receiving your best for my life. I commit my body, mind, soul, and desires to you for purification and sanctification. I pray that your thoughts for me, will become as my thoughts for myself. I know that as I align my will to your will, I will see beautiful manifestations come forth in the desolate places of my life. Your love for me is so extraordinary that you put your son, Jesus, on the cross to die for me. A more powerful demonstration of Love, I don't believe exists. But, I do believe that as you continue to transform me into your image and your likeness, I will be an expression of your extraordinary love to all who I encounter and that as a result, I too, will experience a true extraordinary relationship full of love, support, compassion, tenderness, and reciprocity. I desire this with all my heart and will continue to believe you for it. In Jesus Name. Amen.

About the Author

Kariesha Topping is first and foremost a woman of God, wife and mother of two. As an immigrant from Jamaica who was born and raised in the ghetto, and whose parents instilled good morals and values into, she works hard to persistently achieve her life goals—no matter how big or small. That is how she became a nurse, aspiring entrepreneur, and now published author.

"I love to read books since I was young and it is still my favorite hobby and past-time. I am passionate about the institution of marriage and what it stands for. I love to help others. My motto in life is love, faith, and hope, these three things keep me going."

www.ingramcontent.com/pod-product-compliance
Lightning Source LLC
Chambersburg PA
CBHW062040120526
44592CB00035B/1695